DISMANTLEMENTS OF SILENCE

Poems
Selected and New

WILLIAM VIRGIL DAVIS

TEXAS REVIEW PRESS
HUNTSVILLE, TEXAS

FIRST EDITION

Requests for permission to acknowledge material from the work should be sent to:

Permissions
Texas Review Press
English Department
Sam Houston State University
Huntsville, TX 77341-2146

ACKNOWLEDGEMENTS: The author would like to acknowledge and thank the editors and journals in which these poems—some in earlier versions—first appeared.

The Early Uncollected Poems and the New Poems were published in: *Agni*: "An Early November Meditation," "The Difference between Art and Artifice"; *The Antigonish Review*: "The Swamp"; *The Antioch Review*: "Home from the Factory"; *Arts and Letters*: "A Postcard from San Gimignano," "Rothko's 'Presences'"; *Barrow Street*: "Home Visit"; *The Carleton Miscellany*: "When Things Get Out of Hand"; *The Centennial Review*: "Coming Home"; *The Chariton Review*: "No Time for Welcome"; *Cut Bank*: "Aftermath"; *The Dalhousie Review*: "The Jewel Casket"; *The Davidson Miscellany*: "I-35, South of Waco"; *The Gettysburg Review*: "Near the Cabin," "The Voyeur," "Winterset"; *The Hopkins Review*: "A Cat Named Lonesome," "A Walk Around the Block"; *Long Pond Review*: "Variation on a Theme by Stevens"; *The Malahat Review*: "Letters to My Brothers," "The Tree"; *The Massachusetts Review*: "Ashes," "On a Hill in Crete"; *The Michigan Quarterly Review*: "Alms"; *The Midwest Quarterly*: "Driftwood Summer," "The Hawk"; *The Nation*: "Following the Stones"; *New England Review*: "Pentimento"; *Paintbrush*: "Leaving the Cathedral"; *Poem*: "Confrontation in a Rented Cabin," "The Obstruction," "Small Town on a Winter Night"; *Poet & Critic*: "In Memory"; *Poetry (Chicago)*: "The Pond"; *The Sewanee Review*: "The Last Team"; *Shenandoah*: "The Hunt"; *The Southern Review*: "A Visit"; *Three Rivers Poetry Journal*: "Razing the Set"

Poems selected from earlier collections appeared in: *One Way to Reconstruct the Scene* (Yale University Press); *Winter Light* (University of North Texas Press); *Landscape and Journey* (Ivan R. Dee); *The Bones Poems* (Lamar University Press)

Cover design courtesy of

Library of Congress Cataloging-in-Publication Data

Davis, William Virgil, 1940- author.

[Poems. Selections]

Dismantlements of silence : poems selected and new / William Virgil Davis. -- Edition: First.

pages cm

ISBN 978-1-68003-047-1 (pbk. : alk. paper)

I. Title.

PS3554.A9383A6 2015

811'.54--dc23

2015024625

For My Family

Contents:

Part Five: from The Bones Poems

Part Six: New Poems

I am a fragment, and this is a fragment of me.

—— *Emerson*

I

Early Uncollected Poems

THE POND

I stand above the valley on the old road
overgrown with weeds and mayapple, the ruts
still slightly visible where tractors turned
stones beneath their wheels and gouged out
half-eaten acorns for newer generations
of squirrels to rediscover and carry off
to ancestral haunts in the ancient oaks.

Below me is the valley where I used to play
on Sundays and for two weeks in the summer.
The hillside marches with the raucous colors
of wild raspberries, tiger lilies, poison ivy,
goldenrod, and black-eyed Susan. Brightly colored
birds flit in and out of briers and tall weeds.
Rotten cow dung flakes off a stone at my feet.

I start down the steep incline of the hill,
weaving my way through the thorns which catch
in my clothing, raising choruses of insects,
tearing cobwebs that hang like mirages from my path.
Once I slip, turning a stone over. Tiny grubs
wiggle into soft shadows. The wet face of the stone
blows away in the wind. I reach the bottom

of the hill. One end of the valley has been
barricaded with earth and the natural flow
of the stream has backed up to form a pond.
Frogs loll along the water's edge and splash
away into the dark green reeds as I approach.
An old stump is up to its neck in water. Shadows
beneath the surface glide slowly away from the shore.

It has been ten years or more since I was here.
I recognize only a few scattered landmarks.
The large rock I used to sit on is gone beneath
the water. I select a small smooth stone and
toss it into the center of the pond. I watch it
skip several times before it sinks out of sight
somewhere near the spot where my boyhood rests.

THE HUNT

As if we both had been waiting for this
to happen, I see him
rise up from the hill in early
twilight, his shotgun across his shoulder,
walking toward me
in the even stride I would recognize
anywhere.

We meet at the half-hill. The pocket
in the back of his coat is filled
with a day's quota of small game.
We meet to return together
as if we had set out as one
and taken different directions.
He does not seem surprised,

or ask why I am here.
I turn and fall in with his stride.
The car,
stranded in my childhood, waits
at the end of a meadow
near a small stream. He hands me half
of his take and we bend

to clean the game,
then get into the car. He turns toward home.
We sit and smoke without speaking.
Now I remember that road.
Somewhere out there in the dark
is the place I started from
years ago.

IN MEMORY

(for Martin Jones, killed February 27, 1963)

. . . men feel sorrow, not for the loss of what they have never tasted, but when something that has grown dear to them has been snatched away.

— Thucydides

The smell of oiled air and animals
must have been hot in his nostrils;
the world away, saddled in only dreams.
A pleasure trip, in an army plane,
on weekend leave to show his horses.
In Alaska, between the sun and snow.

Time surely the taste of blue ribbons
and silver saddles and circular rings.
And time between the distances of our
lives and childhoods where we had held
together even over absences. For we
were friends even though time had happened

since we'd played basketball with wads
of paper and the wastebasket in the church
basement, or been to summer camp and
slept together on the ground under
rain and dark, or dated blushing freckled
girls, or talked outside the drama club.

And only now, years later, do I know
the way to say the feelings and the fear
I felt when I heard how he was caught,
as unprepared as I, in the sudden
burst of an exploding plane somewhere
in the midst of a swing into heaven.

THE HAWK

Outspread, he sweeps through
air on extended wings, a flying
feathered cross. And I, looking
up, watch him watching down.

What he seeks is smaller
than I am. To see it he
must see me and see what
even I can't see from closer

range. I can't observe
what must be there. I watch
his fall through shafts of air,
silently, seemingly slowly,

yet with a speed I know
is swift. I fear for whatever
scurries here below within
his ken. Nothing soft could be

safe under his twisted talons,
his crooked bill, his sharp
and steady eye. How many
miles he'd flown, how many

times and miles he fell so,
I couldn't tell by this
descent. I only know I
cowered even though I knew

his prey was something
smaller, something perhaps
more vulnerable than I.
But then he rounded

the basement of air and
rose toward the heavens again.
And a pulse of tenderness breathed
free somewhere, blended in.

FOLLOWING THE STONES

if I could ever really
go back
picking up pieces of shadows
footprints   following
myself through dusty places
over oceans

the breath of animals
accompany me
tongues I have spoken in
break out

cartographer of silences
I speak to the deaf who hear
to the blind   I see
now

how it would come to the same thing
nothing

I chart the last
journey   it begins here
going backwards

stones lead me
everywhere
I am going

AFTERMATH

Gulls slap against the sky, make one last dive,
then disappear. I sit outside the shack
protected by the hill's overhang and wait,
watch the waves erase the land, watch them move
in under the rocks and crash. I add the sound
I cannot hear. I know there is no reason
for you to come back.

                    Still, just before dark,
I see your figure, hunched against the wind,
come up the shore. Wet from the wind and rain
you follow me into the shack. I build a fire,
heat up the coffee, turn on the radio
for the latest report on the storm. Nothing but static.
We sit without speaking, watching the sand spill
in around the leather flaps at the windows.

Suddenly, the storm strikes. Lightning lights
your face, fixed in fear. The flash precedes
the thunder of your scream. All night, whenever
I wake to the twitching of the small ball of your body
clenched tight around the empty bundle
of your arms, I hear you whispering.

In the morning we have to climb out a window
to shovel the sand from the door. The beach
is strewn with the storm's leaving: seaweed,
shells, driftwood, dead fish, broken bones.
The tide out, we walk out to collect the useable
debris, saying how we will make of this piece
of driftwood a lamp, of that a marriage.

ALMS

I remove my coat and put it
around your shoulders.
You pull it close around you.
It was always warm.

My shoes are not new
but they are not worn through.
We wear the same size.
They look better on you.

This shirt, these pants,
they are all I have.
The shirt matches your eyes.
The pants are creased and clean.

The bright belt buckle shines
in the sun. My old cap,
pulled down over your eyes,
cuts your face in half.

You smile but do not speak.
You stretch forth your hand.
I put out my hand toward you.
You take my hand in your hand.

My hand comes loose from my arm.
You stand looking down at it.
It hangs from your hand.
You shake your hand,

trying to shake it loose.
When it comes loose you offer
to give it back.
Finally, you throw it away.

You turn and walk away.
I stand shivering in the cold.
You do not look back or wave.
It has started to snow.

I open my mouth and the silence
sings out of it. I feel it
pull at my tongue, break
over my broken teeth.

I see it spill from my mouth
like balloons, small bunches
of breath. They burst
in the air and disappear.

RAZING THE SET

In the end there is only the wind
and a few bushes blown through the scene.
The façade has been taken down
and carried off in trucks. The cast
has gone long ago. Even the few
extras, a stunt man or two,
several indiscriminate animals
used for background shots, are gone.
The wind picks up. The sand,
like a curtain let down,
covers everything. The place
will only exist if you insist on it.
Not even the night would remember.

LEAVING THE CATHEDRAL

The cold brown dark is half alive.
      The clerestory squints its chinks
of light, which fissure off across
      the floor. The faintest hint
of stale incense scampers out of sight.
      Pale creatures writhe in tortured
fright against the sky. Here you
      and I have stood to stare—
our heads bent backwards—through the glare
      of leaded glass
      and broken light.

Somewhere within the dark above us
      bells bang against themselves.
The muted ring of timeless noise
      pulses through the empty vaults.
Then all is still. The silence grows
      like words. The reredos holds a crucifix.
The altar glows with gold. You take
      my hand. We stop to smile—
then turn and echo down the aisle.
      Outside, we sep-
      arate and go.

WHEN THINGS GET OUT OF HAND

When everything has gotten out of hand
and you no longer know where you are,
when the room begins to close around you,
and the light fades from the windows,
and a flat rain begins to fall on the house,
sit down and try to put your mind at ease.
Turn your memory back to some scene
in the past, force the past to jump
the present and stretch into the future.
Create a dream or call it that, fix it
outside of time. Imagine a place, call up
a face or two, add voices, a few friends,
family, almost anything will do.
Do not give yourself time to think back.
As the rain continues to fall and the room
continues to darken and the shadows lengthen
across the floor, sit quietly. Speak slowly,
quietly. Answer your own questions. Laugh.

VARIATION ON A THEME BY STEVENS

It could have been the color of the sky
or the sound of the ocean in the distance.
It could have been the time of year, winter,
or the lack of ideas. Perhaps it was all

of these, or none of these. It hardly matters.
A girl and a dog are running along a road.
The road is rutted and dirty with snow.
The dog runs; the leash is taut. The girl

runs behind the dog. The dog needs to run.
The sky is overcast, slate. No snow is falling
although it is snowing slightly. The girl
is dressed in dark colors. The dog is black.

As the dog and the girl run they blur together,
into the landscape, into the trees, scrub pine.
The snow, not falling, stops in mid-air.
Thinking of them, the dog, the girl, the snow,

makes them disappear. It is so difficult
to substitute anything. The snow was not snowing.
There was no ocean, no girl, no dog running.
To think of a scene takes the scene away.

THE SWAMP

It was the place we went for play,
out behind the house no one had used
for years. Small, almost hidden in a grove
of trees water logged from the knees
down since the land had been drained,
their knotted roots exposed to the hard sun
of the long summer months. We would wade
barefooted into the dark green water
through the scum, our pants turned up.

Only a few fish remained behind,
with the snakes and mosquitoes.
And an old turtle, large enough to ride,
who haunted the place. We hunted him
all summer long, changing his name
and form to suit our games. For hours
at a time we would crawl through weeds
and rocks, bruising our knees, keeping
to his track in the damp muddy earth.

Like the ghost of the swamp he was,
we seldom saw him. Once he surfaced
in front of us in the water, gulped
a fly or only air and sank from sight before
we could get at him. Again, we traced
his tracks in the mud to the edge of the water
and saw where he slid in, leaving a slick
slide and a trace of tail. Most of the time
we pretended. By late summer the swamp

turned rancid, collapsing together upon itself
to a central puddle of oozy slime.
The moss and algae stuck to the backs
of uncovered rocks and created designs
in scum and stoneworts we would mistake
for the age-old cage of bone the snapper

lugged upon his back. We knew enough to know
better, but never tired of turning rocks
over in the hope of having him in hand at last.

Sometimes it would take several of us
to turn them. The worms and grubs
would wiggle away from the smooth undersides
of the rocks. The damp white clay would belch
and begin to go stale before our eyes. We never
caught the snapper. But once, out all alone
and straining with a stone, I felt as if I had been
given a sign when it fell aside, and leaning
close I saw my shadow swim with worms.

CONFRONTATION IN A RENTED CABIN

There is no need to mention
the ocean. It's always there
in the background.
The sun was low
on the reddened water.
The wind flapped the canvas
I'd fixed to the window.
Sand covered the floor.
The door was open.

Then he came.
When I saw the blur
out of the corner of my eye,
I turned.
He stopped, in the midst
of the trail he'd made,
already halfway across the floor,
pulled in his leathery head
and legs and settled down,
waiting, immovable,
in the center of the room.

So unexpectedly surprised
and out of his element,
he must have guessed
he was vulnerable.
It occurred to me that
it would be a simple thing
to turn him over
and thrust a knife
through the soft bony musculature
of his underside,
between plastron and shell.
I imagined that somehow
he knew, and was waiting for me
to make my move.

I watched without moving.
He was large, old.
Kelp covered his back,
woven into intricate dried designs
with glints of glass
and bits of broken shell
encrusted on his carapace,
and the whole thing
covered with sand and mud.

We both waited.
Then, like a stone
moving up the evolutionary scale,
he extended one leg
and a length of tail.
At last, when he was fully ready
to run if he needed to,
his head inched slowly out,
one eye still closed,
the other blinking, webbed
with a wild watery stare.

Although I was almost scared,
I didn't move.
We stared,
one creature at another.
And then, when we were both
secure again,
he slowly turned
and returned from where he'd been.
As he went, dragging
his ancient watery weight
across the floor,
he erased his earlier trail,
putting another
in its place.

SMALL TOWN ON A WINTER NIGHT

The frozen land is quiet,
the little village closed.
No lights in town are lighted,
no men are on the road.

The men there dream of summer.
The women dream of spring.
The fields fill with wonder,
but no birds fly or sing.

LETTER TO MY BROTHERS

There is not time to remember
what is missing.
We have gown as old
as the apple tree
in the back yard.

I visited it recently.
It still leans
to one side and remains
much as we left it,
although it has lost
one limb to lightning
and another to the saw,
and there's a foot-long scar
on the trunk at about head height.
Lower, someone has taken
several swipes at it
with an axe or a hammer.

As always,
it is thick with blossoms
in early spring
and, later on, bent down
with bunches of small
green apples, the same ones
we made ourselves sick on
every summer.
Like then, the apples ripen,
turn wormy,
fall and are left
to decay, the way
only the ones we missed ever did.

In winter,
in the tree's skeleton,
that intricate cage
of tangled limbs
and the opened circle
above the trunk
where we built our bed
of boards, adding
to it every year,
are signs of the hut
we built and completely enclosed.

But most of what remains
of our presence
is absence.
There are a few nails,
bent and rusted, stuck
in the trunk along the lower
limbs, and here and there
there are still signs
(now almost indecipherable
designs grown large
and shapeless and
partially covered over
with scar tissue)
of the cryptic unreadable remains
of our childhood secrets,
or perhaps just
our blurred names.

THE OBSTRUCTION

An insoluble salt
builds up
around the central
spec of mucus,
fist of calcium,
growing
within the soft
membrane of the gland,
until the sudden
swelling
cuts off the flow
of air and liquid.

It had been there,
lodged at the root
of my tongue,
in the thin
sack of skin
beneath my cheek
for weeks, like
a word I couldn't
quite remember,
haunting my mind,
greedy,
out of place,
but there.

It sends soft pain
through the throat,
along the tensed
tendons.
When I put my hand
to my neck,

it is always there,
as round and hard
as a pea in a pod,
this knot of stone
suspended in my song.

I-35, SOUTH OF WACO

The Ford pickup, painted red but rusted,
straddled the center line. Both back fenders
were dented in.

It was almost noon in Waco. The truck
stalled in the sun, in time, in Texas.

As if in a dream, it began to move forward slowly.

There were three of them in the cab:
two men and a dog.

One was brushing his teeth.
One was drinking from a brown bottle.
The dog was driving.

THE JEWEL CASKET

On a moonlight night in the winter of 1835 the carriage of Marie Taglioni was halted by a Russian highwayman, and that enchanting creature commanded to dance for this audience of one upon a panther's skin spread over the snow beneath the stars. From this actuality arose the legend that to keep alive the memory of this adventure so precious to her, Taglioni formed the habit of placing a piece of artificial ice in her jewel casket or dressing table where, melting among the sparkling stones, there was evoked a hint of the atmosphere of the starlit heavens over the ice-covered landscape.

— Label to Joseph Cornell's
Taglioni's Jewel Casket

Slowly melting over precious stones,
this ice reminds me
of that snowy moonlit night when I was asked
to dance upon a panther's skin
spread over snow.

I did not know the man, nor think
that he knew me. Yet,
I've often paused, as I do now, to wonder
what our little audience
might have meant for him.

It means, has meant, so much for me.
He could have asked for
anything, and gotten it. No one would know. The snow,
new-fallen, soft, filled in the outline
of the trees like flesh

upon the bare bones of the dark.
He'd sent the driver away.
My naked flesh was all alive that night.
I loved to let him watch, his eyes
so soft, so bright,

the panther skin beneath my feet
            so smooth. He stood, his arms
crossed, his face almost averted, the way
        I turn my eyes from these few jewels
                when light catches them.

        I danced for him, or for myself.
                It was as if I saw myself
from some huge distance, or in some great hall,
        at a ball where I was all alone
                in circled center

        place and no one knew my name—
                or knew it all too well.
And when my dance was done, he bowed and thanked
        me with a smile, and then rode quick
                away. The snow

        continued all that night and no one
                ever asked why I
was late arriving. No one has ever known,
        just as they do not know that I
                spread cubes of ice

        upon my jewels and keep a panther
                pelt upon the floor
beneath the open window, and lie awake
        each starry moonlit night to think
                him back again.

NO TIME FOR WELCOME

This is no time for welcome and yet,
there at the door, he stands hatless,
silent and wet, his face streaked red
and black with soot and rain and blood,
his hands stuffed deep into his pockets.

Later, beside a fire, he sits in silence,
his breath halting out in uneven bursts,
like the clock on the mantle, which never
kept accurate time, trying to keep from running
down. After several hours and some sleep,
he rises, still without speaking, and leaves.
Behind him the open door swings rain in.

That night the rain changes to snow. When
you wake and go to the window, the street
is white. Somewhere bells suddenly stun
in the icy air. On the street below your window,
while you watch, no one moves, but there,
imprinting the new snow, footprints appear.

DRIFTWOOD SUMMER

With boards
on our backs
and girls
dug out of the sand,
we walked miles
of water
and sun,
following
the waves.

With bronzed
muscles
and bleached hair,
we ate the air,
devil-may-care
to home
and love.

Evenings,
under the moon,
in the glare
of driftwood flames,
we sang
and slept
and made love
on the sand.

Each new day
we arose,
took up our boards,
and went out
to practice
walking
on water.

THE TREE

Each evening for a full five minutes,
when the light is right, the elm
across the street casts its shadow
upon my neighbor's house.

                                The tree
seems to grow into the house, its shadow
alive in the solid stucco. The leaves
dance within the windows, filled,
fractured, by the wind, the twilight.

For years I never noticed. Then,
one morning, the saws awakened me.
That evening the tree was gone,
cut up and carted off in trucks.

The gap it left created a silence,
an emptiness, along the street:
the presence of the absence of the tree.

That evening, before the darkness fell,
the sky burned brilliant red and gold
and the shadow of the outline of the tree
fell full against my neighbor's house.

PENTIMENTO

It is all there. You stare and stare.
In the lower left-hand corner,
sitting quietly beside a fallen wall,
is the wife you took so long to find.
The tall trees in the background,
blown by wind, half-cover your father's face.
Your dog that died is sleeping
under a broken bucket near the dried-up well.

One of the clouds contains your own face,
turned upside down; another hides
your mother's smile. Your brothers are wrestling
beneath the slow waters of the river.
Your son's laugh is hidden under a stone.
The wind that is moving across the scene
is speaking of all that you have seen,
and whispering your name, your name.

ON A HILL IN CRETE

Knossos stands on a hill
like any other hill here.
Only the goats, those long
years, knew blood puddled
like oil below the ground
where we stand.

                      I take
my son's picture, posed
on the oldest paved road
in the known world. My wife
and son sit in the large
limestone horns above
South House. We view
the huge storage urns,
empty for centuries.

We climb the worn steps
Minos knew by touch and
find ourselves lost
in his famous labyrinth.
The blue stone in the
Throne Room is bluer
than the sky where we watch
an ordinary bird spin high
above scrub cedar.

Daedalus saw this bird
first and pointed
to his son, saying . . .

ASHES

You knew there would be a time for it,
but you didn't know when. When you woke,
fog hung low over the water, hid the hill.
The lights at the end of the yard,
like angels, had haloes. Out walking,
you surprised a squirrel over a black
walnut and watched as he hurried away
to a limb that fell off into air
and disappeared. Then you knew why it all
happened, what it meant, and you reached
into your pocket and took the paper out
and opened it carefully, the folds so old,
the paper so yellowed, so brittle, you
were afraid it would turn to ashes
in your hands. Then the wind died down
and the fog rolled over on its other side
while you read the words out loud, standing
alone in the wide world, waiting.

COMING HOME

Coming home
in sun and shadow in snow
the tree roots tangled in air
the sun as sharp as a razor
and the only word I remember
the only word I call
calling it to the darkness
in this bright sunlight this afternoon
with snow falling slowly
is the wrong word

It rained all morning
the flowers grew old and hung their heads
like prisoners on the last day
I was walking I was lost
I knew it before I knew it

New fields felt old
my feet were wet
the rain grew from the ground
the leaves of the trees
were a false design
the birds what birds there were
flew through the earthy mud
in the dark places
where stones and shadows whispered together

When the snow came
it was no longer the morning
it was no longer the afternoon
it was later than all that
beyond afternoons beyond evenings
beyond walls and stones
beyond shadows beyond dark

Now almost home
how happy it makes me
coming home all morning
coming home all afternoon all evening
past stones and shadows
past rain past snow and sun past words
calling not needing to name

Even from this distance
without a light this deep in dark
without footsteps without shadows
or the shadows of shadows
I know I begin to be there

II

From *One Way to Reconstruct the Scene*

ANOTHER NIGHT WITH SNOW

It is March, 1940. I am not born.
It snows all night. Snow more than a foot
deep between the houses. Trees

holding it along their arms' length.
My father walks slowly home
from the factory, his black lunch box

under his arm, his hands stuffed
deep in his pockets, his red scarf
wrapped twice around his throat.

My mother, big with me, waits
behind the window. Her breath blossoms,
flowers the glass. She has just

put the coffee on. She is anxious
because of the snow, me, my father's coat,
so thin. Last year there was little

work. Now all the extra money, I know,
will go for me. I kick, and turn
over. My mother puts her hand down

and pats me carefully. I see her smile.
She has so much to think about.
The bread wagon comes around the corner

and stops. The horses stamp the snow
and snort over their shoulders. The heat
rises from their haunches as my mother and I

watch them and wait. I think the horses
are wonderful. When my father sees us,
he waves. His scarf blows out behind him.

He is smiling, happy. My mother waves
back, watching him come closer.
He stops to buy a loaf of bread and tucks

it under his other arm. It is still warm.
My father's face is strong. I whisper
to my mother how happy I am.

My father winks at me and kisses my mother.
We stand at the window and watch
the snow fall slowly through the years.

AFTER THE FUNERAL

When the stone falls the water rises up
to meet it, to cup it in its hand and close
upon it like a fist. The ripples spread
outward from the spot where the stone sinks and then
return to calm, and, disappearing, hold
the water level of the pond. After the funeral
I walked the edge of water dropping stones
in the pond. Each time, beyond the blurring, my
face came back together in the mirror
of water, trees grew again, the sky held fast
in place.

          I found a pool off to the side
of the pond. Rock had reared and cut the water
off to leave the pool, isolate and small,
protected by the rock, part of the pond.

Was there some secret seepage beneath the rock
which kept it full? Some private spring? I sat
upon a stone to think things out. Later,
the wind camp up. The trees beside the pond
were bent to the breaking point. The water stirred
and it seemed that, all at once, the pond took life.
Waves, like hands beneath a sheet, began
to move across the lately silent surface.

Then rain came, great droplets. The pond rose up
to meet them, took them in, and lifting from its bed
began to sing. The waves washed against the rock
divide, washed over it and fell into the pool
beside me. They set the puddle moving
with their rhythm and now it rose and fell as well.

And then, all at once, the storm had passed. The sky
cleared, the waves shrank down again and leveled
off. The sun appeared. The rock ridge shined
and dried. The water in the small pool was calm.

I stood up and dropped a stone into the pool.
I waited for the ripples to disappear,
and then I started home. I had learned the secret
of the pool, the borrowed depth which kept it full.

A TRIPTYCH FOR MY FATHER

I

Bent low above the old piano, his eyes closed,
my father leans into the only tune he knows.
Snow catches in the corners of the windows.

The patterned panes are more than half erased
by the intricate embroidery of ice which traces
the glass. The firelight falls full upon his face.

II

On a clear cold morning in late autumn he led
the hogs out and brought the hammer down hard,
in one quick stroke. The ground puddled with blood,

but they fell without feeling anything. The cut
breath, rising slowly from each purpled snout,
caught in the crisp air like an afterthought.

III

This is more than memory. Tonight, unable to sleep,
I sit watching snow fall slowly through the deep
trees outside the window. The fire falls in a heap.

I cannot kill him off. His face is traced in the window,
watching me. The long wind whistles in the old piano.
The room is alive with lost music, in diminuendo.

VIEW FROM THE BACKYARD

Each evening at this hour, birds weave the air.
Birds of all kinds, some so high I can hardly
make them out, faint flutterings, like shadows
moving together to close before they fall.
They make such steady noise, like real silver
spoons clattering in teacups, the old ladies
propped up around the room, their hats on
and gloves, the shades all tightly drawn.

My son, only one year, hears the birds, looks
up, points, says what he says for everything.
My wife says such ceremonies have something
to do with the seasons, the coming migrations,
the getting together of the flocks. It is
as good as any guess I have and so we let
it go at that, not really wanting to know,
knowing all creatures deserve their secrets.

In the darkened room the old ladies speak in
whispers and grotesque expressions take the place
of overt gestures, always impolite. Their hats
are always changing and although no one speaks
of it everyone takes note. The air is heavy
with perfume and stale flower smells. The tea
was never tea and all the old girls are dead.

The circles seem to begin closing in, at each
turn tightening. It is not possible to keep
one single bird in focus while it describes one
sweep of the circle. The sound, with the dark,
increases steadily, by the hour, by the day.
One evening, no doubt soon, when we least expect
it, the birds will suddenly be gone. My son
will stare in vain. My wife will say I told you
so, and turn away. The old ladies in the same
drawing room are dancing on the high-backed chairs.

MY SON IN SNOW

I bring him back from death.
My son, a child of three,
inhabits my mind
this winter day,
caught up in snow.

He is here, playing
in the snow, giving
snow a shape he knows.
His breath blurs and blows
away in the wind.
His snowman stands
in our backyard.

Then the game changes.
He runs and,
twisting in midair,
he leaps and falls
out full upon his back,
winding his arms
to make an angel,
laughing, beginning
to rise. Spent,

he falls asleep
in the snow, his arms
still ready to rise.
I step up to him
and bend down to lift him
from the shape he's made,
his image frozen
in this snow, my mind.

WINTER LIGHT

All night through the dark the dark
is falling. Dead limbs fill with water,
freeze in the hard light of winter.

Out walking this early morning, I stop,
stoop, stare at my own reflection,
bent like a branch is bent by water.

DRIVING ALONE IN WINTER

Driving alone in winter through acres of land
deserted by everything save the snow
trapped in the ruts of the road,
the moon broken by the bare trees,
I remember the days when my brothers and I would fall asleep
in the backseat on the way home.

Tonight, coming home, I remember
the faint light on the dashboard holding my father's face,
my mother's soft voice, my brothers asleep,
the moon running among the trees beside the car.

THE SLEEP OF THE INSOMNIAC

The body beside your body sleeps like death.

There is nothing to hear from your heart,
ghostly clock, full of collapse. Even your
breath, wind from the world's wind, breaks

unevenly, losing itself in itself. Suddenly,

the stars fall to fill your room. Time is
the thin spider you found along the fence
when you were five and kept to yourself

the way, for years, you kept your body

inviolate until you learned there was nothing
to be done for the flesh which would keep it
incorruptible. Death is as close as the wife

you sleep beside. Stars fasten to your forehead.

THE OXYGEN TENT

Always in the dark rooms the sheets
seemed alive. Forced to keep awake,
to keep conscious, forced to watch
the constant rise and fall of the lung
which hung around me like a shroud
(that strange amorphous body breathing
with me) there were times in the middle
of cold winter nights when I believed
I had stopped breathing. Then the sheets
would rise up suddenly and begin
to dance in the dark. Watching them,
I would imagine myself under water,
caught in an airtight, transparent casket,
watching the floodlights splinter
on the dark surface of the water,
draining down to dark above me,
where I waited, out of sight, moving
with the water while they kept dragging
the river, dragging all night, missing me.

THE CAT IN THE SNOW

One morning, before morning, Wallace Stevens,
asleep in Hartford, awoke, several hours before
daylight, and listened to a cat crossing crisp
snow beneath his window. The cat moved almost
inaudibly, he tells us. The fact that Stevens
chose to write about this cat crossing the snow
in an essay on the irrational element in poetry
is irrational, just as poetry itself is irrational.
There is no subject beyond the cat running on the snow
in the moonlight beneath his window, Stevens said.

A LATE ELEGY FOR JOHN BERRYMAN

Admit
that poetry is one of the dangerous trades.
No matter how many we know who have been goaded
by its black promises to deliver
their bodies to the blue snowdrift of death,
it was not poetry, but life, they died of.

—— Peter Davison

Ice floes form on the Chicago River,
passing under the bridges along Wacker Drive.
An old man, hunched inside his overcoat,
the collar turned up, his cap pulled down,
stumbles against the storm, breathing
under his breath some scraps of song.

He struggles against the wind and steadies
himself on a pole, pausing in the spot of light
just long enough to lower his tone and take up
another voice, as if in conversation
with himself. Ahead of him, the red lights
on top of the tallest building in the world
wink at him and he winks back at them,
then continues, more slowly, along the snow-
covered street, as precariously balanced
as a clown walking an imaginary line
through the center of the center ring.
An expert in unease, practiced in his art
and awkward act, he comes toward me
through the snow, covered with snow.
Thinking he might be dangerous, I turn
and cross to the other side of the street.

John, I never knew you, but knew you
were born against yourself. Even your name
against you from the start . . .

I had a student once, old enough to be
my mother, who said, after a reading,
you cried yourself to sleep in her lap.
She knew enough of poetry to know
you were not mad, but she wouldn't sleep
with you. I wish she had.

        The third
anniversary of your death approaches,
like an old man walking above icy water,
staggering against the wind here in
a windy city four hundred miles south
of Minneapolis. The metaphor he makes,
mixed with your memory, has stunned me
into speech.

        The old man continues
slowly up the street, moving through
circles of light. As we are about to pass,
each on our own side of the street,
he stops and lifts his head and stares,
then waves, then goes on on his way.
Thinking of you, even after he has turned
his back, I turn and wave him on.

JANUARY

One morning I awoke and found that it had been snowing all night inside my body. The snow was still falling, filtering down through my ribs, filling in my arms and legs. Already my feet were full. In the left leg the snow was as deep as the knee, as if I had stepped into a hole.

Then I could no longer move. My legs were too heavy, weighted with the snow. When I tried to speak I found my tongue swollen, my mouth frozen shut. It was only January and I had promised to visit a young woman who lived alone in one room above a garage. She had long black hair and never laughed. She must be wondering what happened to me.

SPIDER

The web outside the window filled
with first light, the dew like small rain
stopped to seize the morning. We lie awake
without speaking or smoking. We have been together
this whole night, and never another.
That we both know.
Soon, the spider crouches, still, waiting,
off center but central in the web.
All the lines around him run through
his own wet eyes
and he waits for what the wind will deliver.

THE RING TREE

I see her face in silhouette, against the glass
where light has lightly touched
and wind turned back my mind to this room
I almost remember. On the bureau,
in white, as the room is white, a small china
tree stands, solitary, bare.

There is nothing there. The delicate twig-like limbs
of the tree stretch forth,
as if in winter, toward snow. While
I watch, remembering, the ring tree shifts
in the dimmed light and I see
a young woman's hand stretched toward me.

MEXICO, MY FRIEND

I am thinking this afternoon
of a woman dying in Mexico.

She will not remember me,
although we met once, lived

in the same small town for several
years, had the same friends.

I played poker with her husband,
who usually lost, as he lost her,

although she keeps his name.
I understand that she has married

again. I did not love her
and do not begrudge this fact.

I have never been to Mexico,
although I once hoped to be

a matador. Even this cold
wet afternoon is irrelevant,

I must admit, just a poor
excuse for a chain of words

which have to have some start,
some place to begin to get where

they want to go. In this case,
that is Mexico, my friend.

ONE WAY TO RECONSTRUCT THE SCENE

The moon, through light snow, between the trees,
distorted by the broken glass, looked blue,
almost the color of the girl's blue dress,
or the man's eyes. The car came to rest
against the large maple forty yards from the road,
bisecting the angle of the slow curve beyond the bridge.

The girl was thrown free. She lay as if asleep
against the tree, her hands in her lap.
Perhaps she was dreaming. The man was still
behind the wheel, his hand to his head, a cup
of blood spilled over his yellow shirt. The brake
pedal was pushed all the way through the floorboard.

It was winter. A light snow fell past her window.
She had been waiting for hours. When he came
she had fallen asleep. She dreamed she was dreaming.
He whispered and she awakened. She smiled.
They sat watching snow fall through the trees,
the moon move slowly across the sky. They spoke.

He knew the road by heart. His father had helped
to build the bridge. They were speaking softly together.
The faint blue light reflected from the snow
as it fell slowly through the trees made the blue
of her dress bluer. They did not speak of the night,
no doubt they hardly noticed. There was nothing to know.

It happened without warning. There, suddenly,
outlined in the dark like an animal only visible
when it turns to let you see its eyes, a shape
of something insubstantial cut off his view
as he started to turn, beyond the bridge, just
into the long slow curve. He tried to blink it back.

The girl in the blue dress leaned against the tree.
She seemed to be sleeping. The man remained in the car,
upright, his blue eyes open. Light snow fell slowly
through the barren limbs of the tree above the car.
The moon moved across the sky. It cast a light blue
reflection on the scene, the snow, the broken glass.

THE WEIGHT LIFTER

Only the weight awaits him. There is nothing
to know. He has only one thing to do. Now,
already, he stands over it, breathing deeply,
then bending, waiting, until, in one instant
of motion, in a blur too quick to be seen, he
lifts it above his head, holds it.

                            One summer
he ran with his father through flower-filled
fields, the wind among them, turning them,
his heart in his head, his breath like lead,
his legs lost to only the running, the wind,
the fields filled with flowers, his father.

Blood squirts from one of his eyes but he
does not blink. Instead, he stands motionless,
not thinking of anything, not even the weight.
He feels something small spin around
in his head. He steps from under the weight
and throws it, like a thing, to the floor.

If they ever existed, the fields and flowers
faded long ago. For the old man, alone with
his memories, time is like the broken clock
beside the faded photograph on the mantel.
In the mist of a misty morning he walks
quietly along a lonely road in a white winter.

THE LEAVING

The light lasted on the window,
on the sill. The room was already empty,
abandoned by everything save one gray glove
fallen, fisted and forgotten,
by the side of an empty jardiniere.
The wind blew in from the water
like a landowner. The wagon had been hitched
for hours. The horses stood in the snow
stamping, twitching their ears in the wind.

AN ODOR OF CHRYSANTHEMUMS

Invariably, the room was earthy. There was little
for us to say. We repeated the names, testing our
breath against the odor of chrysanthemums. We spoke
of irrelevant things, not worth repeating. The room
was small, stuffy. The chrysanthemums were yellow
and red. The day was gray, overcast. By afternoon,
a steady drizzle began, as predicted. People we
didn't remember came and went quietly. We spoke
softly and nodded, smiling. Men in dark suits stood
along the walls and blinked when the clock chimed.
Everyone knew exactly what to do. The walls were off-
white. No one spoke of chrysanthemums as inappropriate.

IN A ROOM

It is like smoke escaping through a screened
window. When you enter an empty room,
with a chair in the center, when you
sit on the chair, waiting, and nothing happens,
and no one comes, you begin to notice
the size and shape of the room, the color,
or lack of color, of the walls, the cracks
in the floor beneath your feet, the ceiling
above you. After a time, when nothing
has happened and you have run out of ideas,
you look for the door. When you discover
that it has disappeared you begin to search
for it. You are certain there was a door,
reasonably certain you entered the room
through a door. When you cannot find it,
you sit down on the chair in the center
of the room. You wait for someone to come,
or to call. You notice, now, how the room
has begun to grow smaller, darker.

THAT HOUSE, THIS ROOM

Except for this thin flame the room
would not exist or need to be named.
No one could know, to prove it,
that we were even there. The wind,
in its own windows, rattles what frames
there are. The fire turns a chimney
of wind back to a tree remembering wind,
remembering leaves. The leaves turn
in the wind; the wind catches fire.
You, close, in the chair in the corner,
stir, turn. We both begin to speak
at once. The wind, like a tree on a hill,
begins to burn. There is nothing to know
that house, this room.

CULTIVATION OF PAIN

Put your hand into flame and hold it,
the pain like blood burning, five seconds,
ten if you can. You must learn this.
Call it cultivation of pain.

Practice standing in front of speeding cars.
Test your weight against bridges.
Buy a gun. Depending on your own individual
habits, it will take your whole life
to cultivate enough pain.

SNOW

We are left, finally, to decide why
the world goes, and we with it,
toward some strange kind of return.

This morning, before morning, I dreamed
of snow falling thickly through trees.
When I awakened, snow was falling.

I put on the shoes of separation,
took the road of wandering, and walked out
to find a red heifer unblemished.

I spoke my name to the mountain
and waited to hear a word returned.
Nothing but the wind moved.

In less than an hour my tracks
were covered over, and still the snow
fell thick through the cedars

like dust, dust that at least would rise.

THE TIME OF YEAR, THE HOUR

Snow is falling in the mountains.
For many miles wolves run without resting,
their breath like long scarves of blood.

It is the time of year, the hour,
when things cross and cross again; knock
without knowing they stand before the door.

The fire has found its lost wing,
and the end of the journey, like a shadow
of old shoes, stands waiting to be stepped into.

Water forgets its wounds.
The light has opened its long hands.
Even the dead have stopped dying.

THE PLACE OF LOST BREATH

I have dug a deep hole for the drum
of my heartbeat and put it into the hole
and thrown dirt in upon it and stones.

Later, when I came back to pay my respects,
I found the place only with difficulty
because there was no marker and savage tribes

had set up a circle of fires around the spot
and I had to open a vein in my arm and
show blood to enter again that holy place.

BREAKFAST AS A LAST RESORT

When, some morning, early, at breakfast
upon the patio overlooking the river gorge,
the walls of rock alive in the white sun,
you drop your hand to drink from your coffee
and, reaching, spy beneath the glass-topped table
your feet like boats of death . . .

                    In times like these,
when the world has stopped believing in the possibility
of a future, when there is such energy for evil
which way you turn, there is nothing to do but turn
back to the conversation about the sunrise, the
vistas forward and back, here and there, what
travels you have. Yes, drink from the cup of coffee
and smile at the waitress in the short dress,
who smiles, who doesn't understand your language.

When it is all over and past time to depart,
let the hour ring clearly in the antique clock,
while you hesitate, your hand with the cup of coffee
just to your lips, the end of a sentence brushing
around it. The driver is always impatient, but waits,
whistling, his foot on the running board, cap
tilted over one eye, smiling; he will wait. Place
your empty cup carefully on the ring of its reflection
in the dark glass, straighten your tie, wink
at the waitress on the way out, to the waiting car.

III

From *Winter Light*

FRAGMENTS

At first you think you are still asleep
but the light in the opened window burns
your eyes and the wind has blown the curtain
over the high-backed chair and knocked
the fragile porcelain to the floor. The
fragments lie scattered like fallen flower
petals. This must have been what wakened you.
You lie alone and stare, in this room you
have for only the week, in this place
you never dreamed to be, and think how
strange it has all become. Beyond the window
the steady wind and waves wash the ends
of summer through all your waking thoughts.

LEGACY

In winter, when wind huddled the house,
when snow fell deep and slow, we'd wait
to hear our breath translated back to blood,
trace it all out, over again, an endless
sentence, as if we never knew, hadn't heard
it all before. Sometimes, nights like these,
we remember it again and pile the years,
and burn them back like calendars.

SNOW IN OHIO

In early fall it fell over everything.
The eye of the pond would suddenly
blink shut and stay closed all winter.

The stiff corn stubble froze, snow
fences for field mice. The barren trees
in the small woods, with snow along

their limbs, were like painted post cards
we could keep or send. This was where
we grew. Now the years come and go

and there is no way to account for them.
Memories blur, but I have not forgotten.
This is my mind of winter.

PATHETIQUE

Such a hush, ends and beginnings. All day this music
named me. My ears eyes. It is winter again but there is
no snow. The small house is empty, the wine chilled,
Italian, the bread hard, good, the cheese old, the apples
firm and tart, the best this season. Outside, I watch
the small lake settle through slow mist, still, rising.
It takes me away, the way memories call across long
distances, rehearse all the old terrors. You know, my
brother, what I remember, but I have been waiting here
alone for many lonely years, hoping to tell someone.

THE WATCHERS

The clear bell of the window,
struck by sun, burns clean.
All the edges hold,
this moment, without wind.

Branches pile with new snow.
A single bird, black, holds
against the slate gray sky.
Even the air still, stopped.

This window has worn
the eyes thin, the winter
light burned deep within
my mind. Years turn

and turn again. How old
we are. The window breaks,
falls from the frame.
Last light rings the dark hill.

WINDOWS

The light on the apple is a small window
reflecting the room. In it
I see you staring out over the mountain
covered with first snow.
Here, where summer never ends,
where the world is flat, little changes.
Nothing without notice. I know
you would understand such attention
to detail. I remember you said
you had memorized the mountain, the route
you would take to the top, step
by step. I imagine the snow falling
and you sitting beside your window,
waiting for the precise moment
to begin. When I turn to the window
behind me, only my face reflects
in the fading light.

THE POLAR BEAR

Surfaces from under ice,
glides to the icy shore.
Everything here is white,
absence of all color.

Tests the crust of ice
with his paw, breaking
the edges away, once, twice;
and then begins hauling

himself out of the water,
shedding chunks of ice.
Stands and shakes water
from his fur in white

light. Leaves a track
anyone can follow.
Here the only thing dark
is death. Dark and brittle.

A MAN AND HIS HAT

Once, in winter, half the world away,
I watched a man chase his hat over
a mountain of snow. The wind carried it
continually ahead of him and he ran
through blown snow as if in slow motion.
He would almost reach it, then the wind
would catch it again and lift it off ahead
of him. He ran and ran but the wind kept
the hat out ahead of him. He climbed through
fences, around bushes, through fits of wind
and swirling snow so that, sometimes, I
lost sight of him. But always the hat
blew off ahead of him until finally I saw
him stop, sit down in the snow to rest,
watch, while his hat blew on and on
until it rounded the mountain and was gone.

AN EVENING IN ADVENT

The moonlight has lifted the water from the well.
Along the long road every pebble shows, grows whole.
The corn stubble still stands in its even rows.
Each tree can be seen individually. Everything is still.
This is the kind of night, when we walk out alone,
that we feel blessed, even among our own shadows.

THE LIGHT

It is the most white light.
The dark, like a drawer, has slid shut.
We wait and the nothing happens.

There is no beginning or end.

The key has turned tight and locked.
The mirror on the bureau burns.
We wait and we wait again.

WINTER WALK

The dark comes early.

All afternoon a light snow
fell. Now the moonlight

runs her smooth hand over the land
and the wind whispers above it.

The small sound of my going
reminds me how close

above the dark I go.

IV

From *Landscape and Journey*

LANDSCAPE

How old the dark has become,
standing silent in these fields while
horses weave through each other's shadows.
They have come like warm rain
and run over the hills in the moonlight
and stood so long alone no one
impatient would ever notice them there.

When the wind and the winter return
the horses will still be here,
their silhouettes outlined in the pale moonlight,
standing still and silent on these hills,
or stamping, splattering snow in small spills,
the whole scene turning slowly into landscape
like our own earliest memories.

IN THE COLD AIR REGISTER

Sometimes, when something would fall
into the cold air register, my father
would take me by the legs and lower me
into it. His fingers, locked
like leg irons on my ankles, held me
as I fumbled for what had fallen.
When I'd call, he would pull me,
wet with sweat, my head spinning,
back up into the clear air, into the room
spattered with such bright light.

THOSE SUNDAY MORNINGS

I remember best those Sunday
mornings in winter, with snow
over everything, and the air so
cold it broke like teeth breaking

when I went out to find the
bundles of papers, dust the snow
from them and assemble them,
all the ads added to the center

sections making them extra heavy.
Then to set off along the lanes
of lighted streets, the snow falling
fast, clawing across the light.

I made the same rounds, those
Sunday mornings, that I made
every day, but it took longer,
and it was a harder work.

This was my first experience
with carrying words to people,
but I knew, even then, that it
was what I'd always want to do.

THE OHIO POEM

— for James Wright

1

It is early morning.
Trees lift from the fog the sun
is burning away.
Along the river the Iroquis called beautiful
an Indian stalks the faint imprint
of a twelve-point buck
who moves off ahead of him downwind.

2

I remember the thicket,
the hobo jungle,
where the park ended at the railroad tracks.

Once I touched on old bum
I thought was dead.
When he sat up
I ran the whole way
home,
too terrified to tell
where I had been.

One spring my brother and I
met one of them
at the top of the hill.
He waved and spoke to us.

That afternoon we saw him again.
He was leaning against a tree
near the small stream at the bottom of the hill.
His face was clean. His head rested
lightly against the tree.

He seemed to be asleep.
Unless you looked closely
you would never see
the bracelets of blood he wore.

Later, we tried to remember:
did we speak,
or slip past silent?

3

And now your bones are turning
dark, like emeralds,
burning in the dark wind
somewhere along the dirty Ohio north of Wheeling,
where the women dry their wings.

Gentleman Jim, are you gone?

WINTER SOLSTICE

A pink wash over everything
and the wind down to whisper.
Squirrels stop on bare branches
but blend in so quickly if you look
away you never find them again.

This twilight must happen only
here, only once or twice each year.
I saw it first last winter, black
trees and houses lined up along
the horizon like silhouettes cut

out of paper and set up along
a board in a classroom long gone
into memory, where I first stared
at the shapes light makes on things
and learned I wanted to repeat them.

SCENES FROM CHILDHOOD

1

In winter, when a dirty lace
of snow wristed the walks and driveways,
the coalman came. His truck
shiny black, he backed in
from the back alley, slid his chute through
the basement window and shoveled
the coal into the cellar. For a few
minutes there was nothing in the world
but the rumble of the coal coming in
and the black dust filling the air.

3

The ice, covered with a black tarp
and nested in straw, was cut in huge blocks.
The iceman heaved each block onto his
shoulder like a sack of oats, bending under
its weight. His shiny leather shoulder patch,
strapped over his shirt, gleamed, slippery
with wet. He had a wide gap-toothed
grin and joked with everyone. He put
a block of ice in the icebox in the corner
of the kitchen and, snapping his pincers
at us, laughed his way back to his wagon.
In summer he always gave us slivers to hold
in our mouths. We shivered, loving the cold.

DOUBLE ELEGY

Windows

for my mother, in memory

This small window. I remember my mother,
framed by buds, her breath held, looking for me
in the top of the tree, higher than the house.
We waved and she waited, watching me climb down
through the intricate branches of the old maple
that stood guard at the corner or our yard.

Today I stare, almost level, into scrub oak,
some cedar mixed in, this window years away.
These are the holidays. I imagine my mother
back there, at her window again, watching. What
do we know? Although the seasons have changed
their windows, we watch together. We wave.

For My Father

in memory

I seem to see him often, at dusk, out
near the end of the yard, walking quietly,
alone, into the evening. I watched him

walking there for years before the image
fixed in my mind, became what I knew
I could never forget. Now that he is dead,

his image (something that may be nothing
more than the darkness moving slowly off
at the end of the yard, or coming, slowly,

to meet me) is all that I have left of him.

A VISION IN LATE AFTERNOON

The heat like a hand presses against my head,
and I think I see, from across the yard, my mother,

dead, move past the window of the living room.
Obviously in a hurry about something inside,
she'd only glanced quickly out the window
as she passed through the room and then was gone.

This all happened suddenly, as visions always do.
But now I wonder if my mother might have seen me,
fleetingly, standing there in the yard, as she hurried
through the room. Was she, like me, unsure of what

she thought she saw? Was it too late for her to turn,
to look back over her shoulder? I wonder if my image
materialized for her only after she had already gone on
into the other room—in much the same way that my

vision of her flared and burned, then blurred, in the late
afternoon heat, with the weight of all the years.

OCTOBER: WITH RAIN

The way the light lasts longest on a single spot
of windowpane, some small distortion in the glass
that keeps its final clasp of wind and rain as well,
has caught my eye again. My son has grown so fast
toward man I marvel my own age, try to sort out all
the years, run the film as far forward as I dare.
We sit together at the table, this wintry day
with rain, and do not speak, although I think we think
the same things out, muse on the rain and windowpane,
and in our own ways try to fill the final outline in.

THE RIVER: A VISION

What I saw was a river, a certain slant
of light cut through large leafless trees
bent almost double. That and not much more.
The dark river moved. The wind dropped off
and the trees bent back upright. The sky
blackened and stars appeared. We walked hand
in hand without speaking toward something
in the distance. I don't know what it was
or whether we reached it. That didn't make
much difference. What did seem important
was the river, old symbol for the stream
of time, running swift and dark beneath the
star-struck sky. But this was just a vision.
Why I would want to tell you anything so
indistinct is not clear, even to me. We both
know that I have been wrong about many things.

VIGIL AT HEILIGENKREUZ

The cold comes close around us,
breathes with me.
Do I drowse? In the corner,
near the cracked column,
a young monk slips past so quickly
I almost miss him.
He is late, hurrying to service
with his brothers.
He does not think to look
over his shoulder,
never would have noticed me
sitting half-asleep in the long dark
down the cold aisle
of the centuries
where we both serve.

STAVE CHURCH

— Bygdøy (Oslo)

Even then it must have seemed out of place.
Today, we make our slow wet way up a steep
trail, through evergreens as old as this century,
to a door so low we have almost to bow
to enter. Inside, the air is thick with age.
The dark light does little to illuminate
the small round room, the central wooden
altar, the benches built into the walls.
It is almost impossible to imagine what
it must have been like: the small crowd
congregated here no more than once or twice
a year, sitting without speech in this place
made holy by tradition more than anything
else. We sit and stare and hug ourselves
for warmth. It has the hush of churches
anywhere and I wonder that we make so many
pilgrimages to places like this, often almost
inaccessible, to sit and stare off into
the musty ancient air of other centuries.
What do we hope to find? Our faint faith,
our little service ended, we rise and bend
beneath the door again and track our way
back the way we came, through a snowy trail
of our own faintly frozen footprints.

A VISIT TO MANAFON

— for R. S. Thomas

Still patches of snow on the high hills
above this frost valley where new lambs
run from watching ewes in air so cold
with chill your breath like glassy mirrors
breaks off in front of you and you walk
through your own reflection — think back
through time to more than forty years ago.

The small chapel, built from stone quarried
from the nearby river, has stood for centuries.
The western wall, thick with vine-veined
stone, is a map of the rooted land itself.
In the tiny room at the back of the nave
two small windows — barred since recent
break-ins — hold fifteenth century angels

in pale green and yellow glass. The warden,
from her lambing fields, aproned in mud,
has come to let us in. She watches nonchalantly
as we roam around. There isn't much to see.
"We sometimes have a dozen for services." She
identifies herself as she would be remembered,
"The little girl in the blue dress," and gives

her maiden name to those, like us, who ask
about the past. The great man, when he was here,
we wondered, did she remember him? "Oh,
yes, of course. How could I ever forget? It's all,
now, that brings folks like you. Nothing else.
Yes, he was here for twelve years. He sometimes
came out to the fields when we were bringing

in the hay." "To help?" "Yes," she laughed,
"to help. But he was such a big, strong man.
He threw the hay all the way over the wagon.
Mostly, though, he came at night, to sit and talk
before our kitchen fires. He had a gentle voice,
always spoke softly. But the eyes. That's what
you'd remember, the eyes, like fire reflected;

burning, always burning." We take a quick last
look, sign the book, thank her for opening, then
wander out into the walled grounds, the small
cemetery surrounding the church, through patches
of snowdrops, down the short curve of road, past
the ash tree that unleaved suddenly like a fountain,
to the rectory (now in private hands) beside the river.

.

All is still. Everything is damp. The trees drip.
The hills surround this spot, this hushed hollow.
We have no time to climb above the village,
see from where he saw the rolling hills of Wales
stretch westward toward the sea. It is as if the
silence itself has spoken. Below, the people he
came here to serve; above, his distanced God.

TAPESTRY

Veins and arteries carry the blood from corner
to corner. The interpretation is easy once you find
the right place to begin. The Duke, on his white
stallion, has killed a knight from the invading
army near the center of the scene. Three of his
own followers lie in a heap at his feet. There are
too many corpses to count. A small stream winds
through the valleys, the rolling hills of the
background, done in a flourish of autumnal color.
In the lower left-hand corner, worked intricately
into the dense undergrowth, is the small signature
of one of the women who worked her life away
on the other side of this scene, in the cold tower
where the tapestry, for centuries, has hung.

"LANDSCAPE WITH A POLLARD WILLOW"

—— Hanns Lautensack

The telescoped view
forces the focus through
the foliage, the fingering
limbs, leaving the gaze to linger

on the church, its tower and steeple,
fixed in the center of the scene.
There are no people to be seen,
no animals. There is simply

this scope of the land, etched
as it might have been sketched
on an afternoon walk by one
on his long way home alone.

WINTER ROSES

November: the cold walks stark
in sunlight; the whole hillside
filled with snow. On the small
balcony, you stand and stare.
Your coffee cools in the tiny
china cup beside the marble
balustrade where winter roses
bloom in heated glass containers.
The fragile curtains frost
with fresh designs. It is all
years ago now. You stand alone
and see how unobtrusively
the dark fills up the dark.

POMEGRANATES

The blood-red arils, tart to the tongue,
slash the thirsty throats of history, and men
along long trails and over mountains,
slog through sand as deep as camels' knees
and, whipped by winter's winds, are now
about to turn the corner of another century
somewhere in the deserts of Afghanistan.

Pomegranates cluster close against the house,
near the back door that bangs behind you
as you enter a room of ghosts—who never
fail to recognize you in spite of your ever
more elaborate disguises. The thick-skinned,
several-celled berries brush their reflections
in the windows. We are all eating glass.

POEM ENDING WITH A VARIATION ON A LINE
BY CHARLES WRIGHT

Winter, and sleeves of gray bone hang limp in
the wind. The tortured sun has cut its own throat.
This late in this late century nothing is new

or news. We nod off in the early afternoons
and wake, unrested, to icy feet and fevers.
Under their snowy hill, out of the wind at last,

my parents continue to repeat their prayers
in the same ways that we, with our raspy throats,
try to comfort one another. How many days

have disappeared into dark tunnels? How many
times will we come back to empty cupboards
and drained drinks, to landscape like laundry

frozen on a line? In a bare corner of an empty
room an old spider has spun an awkward web.
The distance between the living and the dead

is no more than one heartbeat or one breath.

A STREET SCENE

When I think of seeing them, walking
down the street, hand in hand, the woman
and the little boy, no doubt her son,
why do I associate this scene, this street
of spring at dusk somewhere in Ohio,
with this strange unrest I feel now,
more than thirty years later? Why do I
let that distant light remind me of, not
something that has passed by long ago,
but something that still lies ahead,
something I do not now know and have
no way of knowing?

                  They were walking
away from me. I never saw their faces.
They did not seem to speak. The woman's
dress, cut loose around her knees, swayed
softly as she walked. They entered the tunnel
of trees. The small boy had to stretch to hold
her hand. He rather bounced along beside her.
Occasionally, he looked up at her and she
looked down at him, but I don't think they
talked. Once or twice, before they passed
from view, they seemed to swing their joined
hands in a little half-arc, and, once,
I'm certain, I saw the small boy skip.

SESTINA WITH TWO LINES BY CHARLES TOMLINSON

Summer thunder darkens: the evening is falling apart.
It is the end of the end of the second season of the year.
We have lived through the apocalypse for too long.
The last doubled rainbow has fallen out of the sky.
Sheep on the rambling hills are eating their lives away.
All the roads in are narrow and filled with potholes.

Once off of the main road we confronted the potholes,
so many that we wondered if the car would fall apart
before we arrived. For years now we had been away,
but we had almost forgotten the intervening years
as we sat there over a cold dinner watching the sky
gather into the thunderstorm, wondering how long

it might be before we could go out again. Not long,
as it turned out. So we drove back through the potholes
and into the shabby town, and watched the darkening sky
glimpse gold and red before the last clouds parted
and everything suddenly went to full dark, like the years
we could hardly remember, the years we had been away.

We took a drink in a small smoky pub but went away
before the loud crowd came. After that it wasn't long
until we were on the road again (now how like the years
it seemed) making our slow way back through the potholes
to the small lonely house. Still, we knew it was all part
of something we had seen fleetingly in the dark sky.

When we arrived back, there was nothing left of sky.
The whole landscape seemed to have gone far away.
We climbed up to our room, acting our proper parts,
without speaking, and I wondered if you were longing
to get away again, even if we had to deal with potholes,
even if we didn't know where to go with the years

left to us. I guess we both knew by then that the years
would be shorter, and that even the most spectacular sky
was short-lived and filled with its own kind of potholes,
and that, no matter how we tried, there was no way,
really, to get away, no matter the miles and the longing,
no matter the weather; and that we all had our parts

to play, and that all the parts were filled with potholes,
and no matter how long we waited, how many years,
a dark sky would lead us on; that there was no other way.

FIRST LIGHT

— for R. S. Thomas (in memory)

I climb the steep stone
steps, glassy with cold,
to enter the empty church.
Faint light swords through
the upper dark. No wind
murmurs. No candles burn.
No God waits there nor wakes.

Last night, quite abruptly,
it began to rain. And then,
before morning, the rain
turned slowly to snow. And
then again, before first
light, almost imperceptibly,
the snow turned back to rain.

A NIGHT AT THE MOVIES

The film already fifteen minutes old,
their awkward line was ushered in by hand.
I wonder what it was that they'd been told?

They stumbled down the aisle as shy and bold
as children lined in lines, hands held in hands —
the film already fifteen minutes old.

Their leader led them to the front and scolded
them to sit and stare and try to understand.
I wondered what it was that they'd been told?

And then one old man, out of all control,
stood, and started to talk — to comprehend —
the film already fifteen minutes old.

Five minutes later, still staring over their shoulders,
their leader led them out, held hand in hand.
I wonder what it was that they were told?

Since then this scene has folded and unfolded
again and again in the darkened room of my mind.
The film is always fifteen minutes old.
I wonder what it was that they were told?

COURTYARD LOOKING TOWARD ARTEMIS FROM THE WEST CLOISTER

— Isabella Stewart Gardner Museum, Boston

Unarmed Artemis, your mouth
opened in awe or slight surprise,
you stand surveying the scene in

this most modern garden. Centuries
spin before your sightless eyes while lilies
ring their silent bells. Frail ferns

and cineraria whisper softly
in the stone-stilled atmosphere.
We wander among the squared-off

rooms surrounding you, turning
over in our minds thoughts we thought
we had forgotten. Each turn brings

back to breath the beautiful,
the true. Then we return to you.
Demetrius of Ephesus, your fears

have proven false. We stand and stare,
and wonder if, in our modern world,
when we return to it, our being here

and seeing you will make much
difference. We walk out into the world
to do what we must do.

POEM BEGINNING AND ENDING WITH A VARIATION OF A LINE BY GEOFFREY HILL

I stray amid the things that will not stay.
I look at you and watch you look away.

It seems we've both been here before,
although we can't remember when. On the shore

three gulls eye us warily, then haughtily stalk
off. We have given up even on small talk.

We climb the steep path, through stepped sand,
to the ruined castle. In the keep we take our last stand

and stare out over sunset-ribboned water. All day
we've strayed amid things that we know won't stay.

SOMETHING I CANNOT NAME HAS COME CLOSE TO ME

In deep waters blind fish struggle
toward lines not yet let down.

NOVEMBER

And has it now come to this, this
autumn room, this sitting in silence,
waiting for whatever it is to arrive,

to this certain uncertainty? The light
opens the window and bars me in.
Even the words on a page, read

relevantly, read slowly. Although
I remember much, some things,
now, seem difficult to remember.

I must trust that all that needs recall,
I will recall. It is almost noon. I am
waiting for someone to arrive. He is late,

but I have always been patient,
and so I will wait, watch the long
afternoon shortening its shadows,

listen to the few birds singing,
the old clock ticking, see the last
leaves flutter from the stoic trees.

PILGRIMAGE

We never knew the way, couldn't get there
for the going. All day the sky had been grey
with a light mist falling. Not knowing what

we were looking for or finding had found,
we were anxious to finish whatever it was
we'd begun, to have this day put away,

on the calendar, in the album, where if we
wanted to we could take it out later and
examine it — fixed, unchanged, framed,

defined, a piece of history, even if our own.
It comes to this: we choose the life we live.
For years now I have been carrying one

small smooth stone to a nameless shrine.

DIET

I wonder what you must have been like
at sixteen or seventeen—beautiful,
no doubt, but even then (those terrified eyes)

afraid of what you knew you didn't
know, of what you guessed and what
you kept at bay——the way you kept

the boys away by asking them to come
close, come closer. It is still all there
in your eyes, but I am old enough to know

such tricks, the way you've teased life
itself into a corner, like a cat a mouse,
playing with it—thinking at any time

you could end the game any way you
wanted. You ate words for the sake
of poems and swallowed them so hard

it hurt to watch. Now you have grown
thin. You take a cracker or two for lunch,
nibble several bites for dinner. We never

talk of anything edible. You wear the
same suit you wore thirty years ago,
the day I first saw you—all in black

in a stark white room, reading with such
a hush we all held our breath. Your words
echoed in our heads as if they were our own.

But, then and now, you never noticed
us, or anyone else. Now, I want to say
gorge yourself, my dear. Get up

in the middle of the night and raid
the refrigerator. Go out for an early
breakfast. Have a large lunch at a deli.

Do this every day, for weeks, months.
Eat. Eat everything. Do not let me hear
from you again until you are fat—

you who have always been famous
for your metaphors of starvation.

CALL

You know, she said,
he used to call me
maybe six or seven
times a day, interrupt-
ting anything I was
doing, he didn't care,
and it was always
something small he
wanted, to ask a
question or to tell me
something he was
thinking about, or
what he had heard
on the radio he
listened to all day
long, and I got angry
with him often and
once I even said
I didn't want to hear
about it, or from him,
again, I'm tired, I said,
of listening to what
you want to tell me,
why don't you do
something, or call
somebody else,
even though I knew
he had no one else,
and that he often
called me because
of that, that he was
lonely, although
he never said so,
it wasn't his way,
maybe he didn't even
know it himself, or

think about it that
way, it made me
wonder, and I do
wonder what he
did all day long.
sitting there in his
chair, all alone,
listening to the radio,
and maybe thinking
how he might call
me, just to hear
a live voice, just
to talk back to
somebody, and
then maybe he'd
think he shouldn't
call again so soon,
and then wonder
when he had called
the last time, and
not know for sure,
and put his hand
on the phone and
almost dial the full
number, and then
put the receiver
back on the hook
and plan to wait
at least another
hour and then,
when he did call,
he must have heard
the disappointment
in my voice and
maybe he even
imagined all kinds
of things about
himself, or me,
and wondered,

when I told him
I had things to do,
or somewhere to
go, whether I was
telling him the truth,
because he knew
what my life was
like, that I didn't
do very much,
and rarely even left
the house myself,
but we never talked
about that, we never
really talked about
much of anything,
we talked talk, and
then we hung up,
often with some
excuse neither
of us believed in,
and now, every
day, I sit here
alone, and I wish
he would call.

THE OTHER

If he'd known she was watching
from the window in the building
across the street he might not
have been so nonchalant with
the waiter or have waited until
the entrée arrived to take her hand
in his and place it on the gloves
he had given her the week before,
a gift he still had no real knowledge
of with respect to her deepest
feelings about them because she
so seldom said exactly what she
felt about anything. This, he thought,
was one of the major differences
between the woman across the table
from him and the other one.

As he thought of her he turned to
glance out of the window—almost
as if he'd felt a pair of eyes on him,
warming his face the way his hand
was growing warm as he and she sat
staring at each other over a fancy
dessert neither of them really wanted
but both had ordered because they
each thought the other did, and as
the light in the window, darkening,
seemed to signal a turn, like the turning
on of lights within a room, or all along
the street outside the window, or
in the windows all along the street.

WHAT WE SAID

There wasn't any way to know
most of it for sure, and it wouldn't
have made much difference anyhow.
So what we said, the way we told
it, was as good as any, since truth
can't ever really be found out or
untangled, the rope finally thrown
away with the knot still in it. So
what we said was that she must
have known him, must have let
him in because there wasn't any
sign of forced entry, no broken
windows and the only door locked
from the inside. He wasn't some
sort of magician or shape-changer
who could slip in through the chimney
or come in under the door like
smoke or empty air, appear or
disappear at will. He probably sat
there talking to her for a while,
and she might even have given him
something to drink because there
were two glasses in the sink, and
two cups too, but, without fingerprints,
it will be difficult to know anything
for certain. Maybe the autopsy will
tell us what she had to eat or drink,
and maybe not, if it was only liquid.
Anyhow, they must have walked
to the bedroom together, even if
she'd had too much to drink, and
she'd folded some of her clothes,
as if she was waiting for him, or,
maybe, that was when he came
in, interrupting her while she was
undressing, after waiting, watching

her from the window over the fire
escape, the one window unlocked
and still open a crack when we arrived.
So what we thought was that there
might be fingerprints on the window
sill or somewhere else in the room,
or on one of the glasses in the sink,
or somewhere where we least
expected them, but we didn't find
any prints anywhere—other than
hers which, of course, were everywhere.
Her eyes were open, a beautiful
blue, and she looked only slightly
startled to be staring so, as if she'd
been surprised by death too, or
hadn't expected it, or only seen it
coming when he came too close,
and she probably thinking of
something else, something totally
different, and only then, at the last
instant, saw it for what it was,
and saw it was too late, and maybe
she started to smile at that, realizing,
and then stopped, just as she died.
So what we said was that it looked
like love gone wrong, a real accident,
something totally unintended.
Still, she had only been in the city
several weeks and as far as we
knew she hadn't found a job or
had much time to make new
acquaintances or find friends,
and we know she hadn't known
anyone here before, in another life
so to speak, someone who might
have been watching or waiting
for her, someone who had followed
her home, a secret admirer,
or even a former friend she'd be

happy to see when he arrived,
even unexpectedly—someone she
would have welcomed in to talk
about the past they had had together,
or the place they both were from,
or to catch up on old news. We
knew that, most likely, many
of the things we imagined were
things we would never be able
to prove, that most cases of this kind
are never solved. But we always
try to do our best, and, therefore,
if anybody asks, you can tell him
that this is what we said.

AN AFFAIR

When he discovered it
he discovered almost
immediately that everybody
already knew about it.
But nobody had told
him—not surprisingly,
he thought. He knew
he would not have told
anyone either, if he'd
known about something
like this, not even his
best friend, not even his
wife. Indeed, he wondered
how one, really, *would*
go about talking about it?
In this case, wouldn't it
be obvious that (if not
everyone) some at least
would have already
known and, therefore, it
would seem that they
would have assumed
that he knew too—and
thus not tell him—because
(they'd also assume)
either that he knew—
and was trying to ignore it—
or, if he didn't, that he
wouldn't *want* to be told?
They must all, he thought,
have thought that he knew,
thought that he was being
adult about it (not, surely,
that he didn't care, but
just that he didn't care
to discuss it). Even she,

he thought, must have
thought he knew, since—
after the first few months—
she never made any attempt
to hide it from him. Even
so, she must have wondered,
as time went on, when *he*
might mention it, how he
might bring it up, under
what circumstances, where
they might be at the time.
Knowing him, she imagined,
if he *were* to bring it up, it
would, inevitably, be at the
most unlikely moment,
and under the most awkward
circumstances. Early on,
she'd even thought about
what she would say, how
she would defend herself,
even if she would deny it all
outright (in spite of all the
obvious, incriminating,
evidence), or—if she'd been
caught off-guard—might
attempt to throw the blame
back on him, accuse him
of having forced her into it
(even subconsciously)
for some sort of strange
psychological need
he had, and had,
perhaps, repressed.

But, as time went on,
and he didn't say, or do,
anything, and because she
couldn't really be certain
that he really didn't know—

unlikely as such an assumption
was—she stopped thinking
of possible excuses, stopped
inventing various, almost
plausible, scenarios to
cover herself, or even, she
thought, to *protect him*—
if it came to that. And,
therefore, the new became
old all over again, became
a justification for both
of them: he, waiting for her
to get bored with her lover
and come back to him,
to confess—contritely,
he hoped—and be forgiven,
so that they could make
up, and take up where
they had left off; she,
for him to say something,
do something, take some
sort of action, hint at least
that he knew—or, at least,
suspected something—
even, she thought, take
up with another woman,
and thus give her both
an excuse for continuing,
something to throw up
to him—if it ever did
come out and she needed
(as she knew she might)
some excuse. But both
of them, no doubt, knew
that neither would do
either—or both both.

One of the things, finally,
that most intrigued him

was the way he had,
apparently, *permitted* it all
to happen, the way he
had pretended to himself
that it wasn't really
happening at all, that
she was not away,
so many days, on some
trumped up trip, but
actually upstairs, in bed,
asleep, or, even, waiting
for him to come in and
surprise her—even to
make love to her. Had she
noticed, he wondered,
how often he had,
apparently purposely,
chosen to miss something,
overlook an obvious
clue left unaccountably
behind, failed to initiate
a comment or make an
accusation when there
seemed to be an obvious
opening or an
unaccountable gap in
one of her accounts (an
hour or two here or there
left out and open to
question), when she had
given him an almost open
invitation. It was as if,
she thought, that he had
almost *forced* himself
to be deceived—even
as if he wanted to be
finally.

They had,
of course, both thought
it all through many times,
and they had both come,
independently, to the
same conclusions, again
and again, so that all that
ever surprised either of them
now was that they couldn't
seem to get back to
any kind of beginning
beyond this end.

"BORDER VIEW, HOT SPRINGS, TEXAS"

— for Don Neyhard

The house no longer exists.
The outline of a galloping horse
to the right of the doubled
window without glass, the
fist-sized hole just ahead
of the horse's head, are all
long gone. This window into
another world—these hills,
the small white stucco house
in the distance, stunned by sun
and overhung by fog or mist,
floats into my vacant room
of mind to remind me that
everything can quite suddenly
disappear into landscape.

V

From *The Bones Poems*

PROEM

they begin the journey back to the flesh

they stand alone in the wind
and the wind
clothes them with words
and the words
break out on the silence
as if reborn

to speak to those who are still in their skins

AFTER CENTURIES

after centuries
the arms
have come free

they put their hands
to their heads
find the tucked-in end

and begin

to unwind
the bindings

they loosen
some of the bandages
then rest

stretch   relax

they stand
near a door

white light
as fine as dust

the color of blood

seeps

under the door

puddles
beneath their feet

THEIR ARRIVAL

they come
old and young
one from east of the wind
with a burlap
bag on his back
and his head
hung down
on his chest

another
from west of the moon
with a long
white beard
and a lightning scar
across his arm
and a lame leg
so old
so used to the dark
he has lost his shadow

three or four
arrive at night
creep into camp
and fall
asleep
in a heap
by the fire

two come
together arm
in arm
holding
each other up
laughing
drunken
one bottle between them

stumbling in
as much on instinct
as memory

for hours
days
weeks
months
who knows how many
years
too numerous to name
they arrive
in hordes
herds
flocks
some straggling in
alone
or two or three
at a time

coming
from under stones
stepping out
of trees
rising up
from rushing waters
with every waft
of wind
so many
so various
too many to name

they come
as if
to begin again

THE BONES MEET THE BONES

under cover of dark
the bones move between the trees
step silently
over twigs
stones

walk on water in the long moonlight

no one would know they were there

and then
from the other direction
coming toward them as inevitably
as death

the bones come striding

alert in the moonlight
as clean as rain

the bones meet the bones in a small meadow

they walk up to one another like old friends
and fall on each other's shoulders
and weep so loudly

even the wind stops to listen

IN THE PIT

in the pit
in the deep dark of the earth
where there is no light
where even the wind whispers
and only the oldest stones
dare to speak
blind worms
move slowly over the bones
and create
with their intricate embroidery
a moving tapestry
the model of a mind
articulately arranged

THE BONES DIE AND GO ON LIVING

death was so strong
it made them vomit

then they fell asleep

an underground wind blew through them
chilling them
they shuddered in their sleep

they didn't know about death

when they awoke
freed of the flesh
of the thin sack of skin surrounding them
of the stale smell of dried sweat

they didn't know where they were

a chill morning wind
burned through them
and they
shuddered again

the sun began to burn
warming the water
warming the stones

they took a deep breath
and sat up

adjusted their empty eyesockets
to the dimmed light
and looked around with wonder

they stretched
they struggled to stand

then they began to understand

they stepped up

out of the hole
took one tentative step
or two

they walked
they ran

once or twice they fell
but they picked themselves up

they were so happy they could not contain themselves

when they couldn't find
their shadows
they knew they were invisible

they laughed out loud
they answered their own hollow echo

in the years that followed
the bones
had many adventures

some of them
too terrible to tell

some will be remembered forever

some are written here

FOLLOWING THE BONES

the bones do not remember the soft skin
that surrounded them

they pull the dark blood from the skin
and stand up on their own

they walk in the shapes of shadows
and shine in the dark wind

follow them
even though you do not know where they are going

THE RECOGNITION

when they bend
close

to the earth

their shadows
fill

with flesh

THEIR ODYSSEY

three days without water
or shelter
with only the stale wind
for companion

they begin slowly
to move forward again
sand spilling
from the holes in their skulls
blowing through their ribcages
grating in crevices
of knees
and elbows

every step
a strain

even at night
they burn in the burnt black wind

but still
they move
leaving no footprints
alone and lonely
the sand
as wide as their eyes
extend

on the fourth day
they fall

then they begin to crawl
blinded
by sun and sand

mirages
appear in thin air

they smile
and hurry ahead
on the sixth day
living by now
on sweat alone
they drag themselves
over the sand
their breath
halting out

at night
against their will
they roll themselves up in a ball
and fall asleep

tongues of wind
whistle above them
and through them

before morning
almost fully covered with sand
they dig down deeper
seeking sleep
some end
to their ordeal

suddenly
the wind stops

the hush
loud

they stir
stand
begin to move forward again

each step an ache

they totter
they almost fall
move slowly

something they see

in the new light
they drink
the dark
away

IN THE DARK

they root in the dark
send out feelers

find soft damp places
where water waits

where thin strings of light
penetrate

they begin to grow

move darkly
up their own dark veins

like vines
alive

seeking sunlight
and life

even though life
was what they died of

THEY MAKE LOVE

they are stripping off skin
letting it fall to the floor

naked
they switch
the lights off
and clash
in the dark
like armies

all night long
the sparks fly up
from them
burn away
in the wind

it is as exciting as death

AFTER THREE DAYS

after three days without water or shelter
alone on the empty sand
with only the stale wind for companion

when anyone else would have given up

the bones grit their teeth
spit at death
and drink away the dark

THEY GATHER TOGETHER

those that were broken by life
are made whole

those who lost limbs
have their limbs restored

those born deformed
remain deformed

but no one speaks of it

they gather together in the early light of morning

they begin marching
move in turn with a silent song

they gain momentum

they maneuver to let the others in
amending their ranks
as they go

they are singing
their ranks swelling with their music

TRESPASS

if you step in their shadow
even though they are still asleep

they stir awaken and rise
as if from death

they bless you for your trespass
put their arms around you

cold cold
kiss you

your body begins to burn as if with desire

and when you go off with them
there is only the one shadow

and the bones and the bones are still asleep

MEETING THE BONES

the bones are drunk again
as night falls as shadows
step into shadows and the bells
in the old church tower announce
midnight you hear them coming
before you see them they stop
to rest every few feet
fall against lampposts trip
over curbs moving slowly
into view they lurch
down the dimly-lighted street
in search of sleep

just as you are about to collide
they step aside to let you pass

the next thing you know
you awaken behind a row of bushes
not far from a small circle
of light at the edge
of a park a policeman
stands over you his flashlight
bent to your face the faint
fall of a fountain overflowing
in the distance he bends
down to test your breath and asks
you your name and where you live
he asks you what happened
you fix your face in a smile
and tell him you don't remember
the bones inside you are laughing

WHERE THE BONES MOVE

when you move
your bones move
below you
under the earth
stalking
the footprints
of your shadow

as if you were walking
on water
your form
reflecting
beneath the water
head down
in the dark
currents
where the bones move

when you bend
close
to the earth
putting your ear
near your ear
your heads together
your feet treading
water and air
you hear
the dark words
seep
from your skull
grow
upward beneath you
lodge
in your mind

as you walk
you listen

you speak to hear

then
listen again

you run
following the bones

they run
following you

you are old friends and enemies

it has been
too long
since you've seen
one another

since
you have sat down
together
and talked

in the dark hours

THEIR SLEEP

when you sleep
they walk out in the dark

all night
restless

they hike hills
wade rivers
flame in the wind

with dawn
they turn and return to your bed
take up your skin
and step off again

muffled

invisible

AFTER DARK

at night
as you enter your dream
the bones get up from your bed
to take their exercise

they step from the bedside
walk out
through the wall

they jump the garden fence
and whistle away

creatures of habit
and necessity
they keep to the alleys
taking their usual walks
following their typical tracks

they take a few turns
around a long block
moving like shadows
through dark alleys
behind houses

dogs tied up to watch
and give warning
do not bark
they know them
by sight and smell

the bones feed them
and the dogs lie down again
go back to sleep
on their paws

they walk
to the edge of town
and out of town

they travel dirt roads
no one sees
how they gleam
in the dim moonlight

they always stop
at the cemetery
for an hour or two

then
before morning
when the first faint light
brushes the sky
and their shadows
fall in front of them
they turn to return

they follow the same routes
summer and winter
in spite of the weather

at last they climb in
through the window again
step to the side
of the bed and lie back down
with you
shaping their shapes
to the shape you are sleeping in
and if you are dreaming
they dream
your dream with you

you have never known
them not to return
not to be there
to greet you

when you awaken

SOME THINGS THE BONES NEVER KNOW

when you sleep
they think you have died

when you awaken
they believe in miracles

when you hide
they look for you

when you die
they are born to the air

they say
where did he go

THE BONES IN SEARCH OF A BED

a hand comes up the banister
outside the bedroom door
they hesitate
the wind hushes
under the door
and the angle of light
opens slowly

you slide over the side
of the bed
and pull myself in
under it

the bones
stop beside the side
of the bed and the bed
takes their weight
like a shadow disappearing
in the dark

they stretch out above you
adjusting their shapes
to the shape you made
in the sheets

beneath them on the dusty floor
you fall asleep
in the empty sack of your skin

RENTING YOUR BED TO THE BONES

you have rented your bed
to the bones
they came saying they needed
a place to sleep
all night you dug in the dark
working your way around stones
pulling up roots of trees
clearing the plot
at last the earth opened
like water
when the hole was wide enough
and deep breathing
evenly in the dark air
the bones stepped
into it like owners
and lay down
they shifted their weight
slightly to find
a comfortable rest and then
fell asleep you covered
them over with the soft earth
and left the rent
will not be due for years

THEIR WORDS

their words
keep

composing

decomposing

the names
of your name

THE BONES COME HOME

for more than a mile
the bones
like a basket of junk continually collapsing
have been following you

you try hiding in doorways
running down darkened alleys
cutting across lawns

they stop when you stop
move when you move
their awkward gait
insistent
not to be denied

at home at last
you enter the darkened rooms
step out of your shadow
and begin to climb the stairs

you hear them stop outside the door
hear the door open

and the night air come in with them

at the top of the stairs
you turn and see them standing there
below you
just beyond the landing
balanced against the banister
waiting for you to turn
to continue

when you get to your own room
you station yourself
behind the door
and wait

you hear them stop at the top of the stairs
to catch their breath

then
breathing evenly again
they make their way along the long hall

they enter your room and
hesitate
as if they needed time
to adjust to the dimmed light

then they step to the side of your bed
standing between you
and the light
which shines straight through them

their empty eyesockets
fill with fire

your eyes begin to burn

IN FAR FIELDS

in fields far from home
the bones are eating rain

free of the flesh
they rest in the damp earth

as the sounds of life die out
as they dream their favorite dream

they have already forgotten your name

THEIR DEATH

they never die

OIL

they add like oil
loose their own designs

fall into heaps

the heaps begin to grow

they dare the wind
to stop speaking of them

THE PROMISE

and if one day they will rise
do not let the light know
or the ground which covers them
which was always warm
or even this song they sang
this sad long song no
do not let it know

let it come if it comes
like unexpected water when roots
are dry like lightning
in a calm summer sky
or animals new-born stepping out
on new-fallen snow or
breath where no lungs are

AND IF SHRIVEN AT LAST THEY RISE

and if shriven at last they rise
and their parts report as promised
and fly through the air
to sing like some winged instrument

then let it be like the breath
they took and gave in life
like the rivers of air they drank
or the death they died to

without pain or pause
unnoticed until it was over

NOT MANY YEARS

not many years from now
when they dig through the debris
they will find a stone
among the bones
and not knowing what
they are looking for
or finding have found
they will throw it away
never realizing
how deep the bones dug
to find the stone
never stopping to listen
to what it is whispering
or see when they smash it
how the light
splinters

THEIR DEPARTURE

and then one morning
before morning
the dew still heavy in grass

even before birds

slowly
they rise
yawning
covered with frost

as if new
or newly born

their joints creak and crack in the wind

silently
they step together

quietly
take their places

speaking softly

they stand
beautiful in the sunlight
fingering them

turning them golden

in the wind
blown through them

slowly
they walk off
together

two by two

into still darkened distance
singing as they go

not yet out of sight
dancing
the line of them moving
dancing
as far as the eye can see

in no more than a moment
they are gone

without even an echo

and the air
is empty again

and the day
dawned

INTO THE DARK

like shadows
within shadows
they glide
from tree to tree
moving off
always
ahead of you

they glance
back
over their shoulders
and smile
their teeth
gleaming
in the moonlight

they turn
step off again

beckon

you follow them

moving further
and further

into the dark

GROWING DARKER AS THEY DEEPEN

growing darker as they deepen
like water seeping
through holes only worms
could find

they twist and turn

and if at last they rise
like water sprung from rock
or water sprung from water
they rise the way they were

from shadow into shadow
as silently as skin
grafts on to skin or bone to bone

dying to be born again

AT REST

now the bones are at rest

no one need know where they have gone
or what they dream to do

the bones are at rest content

perhaps they are dead
perhaps they are only asleep

perhaps they will never return

for now anyhow it is over
this endless emptying this filling

so much like what we name breath

VI

A Selection of New Poems

ROTHKO'S "PRESENCES"

(for Bill)

The huge ones are rooms we live in;
the years alone; when we die.

Black on Grey (1969)

things grow deep in deep waters
yellow and green yellow and green

of course it is dark the sky
full flat black

floats on the water
nothing is gained or lost

or everything is

Black, Pink and Yellow Over Orange (1951-52)

another black sky above a thin
white horizon and the bright light
of yellow fields over an orange

background rain fringes the left
side a small red dot has been blown
through the black by a large

funnel-shaped horn the central
band of pink like a lake
or nothing reflects

along the top of the yellow
the scene is bordered in orange
orange orange is everywhere

Number 18 (1951)

white light a red-orange horizon
above all the blood
many men will die in the blinding light
no one is raised from the dead

this painting will fill the whole room
flow over the wall guests will sit
speechless under it will stare
stare purple pink blue red

Untitled (1969)

black sky above swamp
an arm reaches up hand holds something
like a log with one eye

something swims near the bottom
not even water or the sky

covers everything
nothing traces
around us all her white spaces

Light, Earth and Blue (1954)

it is more than half light
yellow thin white ghosts
stand sentinel at the center

the earth aquamarine above
a deep blue sea is an old
world still

in all elements
you can venture over edges

Orange, Red and Red (1962)

a field on fire
the land less than the sky

the shadow of your watching head
thumbprinted at the bottom of the picture

it is better to run forward
through the fire

Untitled (1954)

a window or a door

if window closed
door closed
no handle anywhere

glass frosted over
this is a mirror

see what you see you

Black on Maroon (1958)

are these your parents walking toward you before you are born

the one on the left your father slightly
taller rigid and silent the other your mother

a bit behind less clearly
defined the outline fuzzy

they try to tell you everything you'll ever need to know

Grayed Olive Green, on Maroon (1961)

a red casket
grey-green ground all around

the sky and the land
the same

the casket empty
waiting for you

Black on Black (1964)

degrees of death the outline
outlines itself you step

to the edge to step to the edge

                stand totter
            adjust your eyes

black black black black black

HOME VISIT

He sported a razor cut
on his neck at breakfast
and, when I asked, said,
"You never taught me

to shave with a blade."
Once again, he'd outrun
my attempt at interference—
as if spotting an opening

from the corner of his eye,
he'd cut back against the grain
heading for an open field
ahead. I smiled, remembering

well the misty bathroom
mirror and the lather dipped
from my father's shaving cup,
red with my young blood,

and the way one opening
opened up the whole field
as I ran quickly through
an early autumn afternoon,

the end zone clearly in view.

A CAT NAMED LONESOME

— in memory of Weldon Kees

The cat and a pair of red socks
soaking in the sink was all
we found in the apartment.

In the car, parked carefully
close to the side of the street
not far from the end of the bridge,

the keys were still in the ignition.
That was it—no note, no word
to anyone. No plans that anyone

knew of. And the day was like
most days in San Francisco,
the fog like a lover hovering over.

A POSTCARD FROM SAN GIMIGNANO

— for my son

*There are these fragments of words I picked up on the hither
side of my limits. I am sending them to you, because you will
love them. Consequently, you will know to piece them together
into a vision of your own design.*

— James Wright, in a letter to his son from San Gimignano

We have grown accustomed to see presence
in absence, loss as gain, the unspoken or unsaid
as the most intense, most fully remembered,
to discover that it is almost always what is
missing that means the most to us,

                              the way
a pause in speech fills with silence to
speak more loudly than words, or a lost
appendage, or a broken statue, mends in
the space where a missing arm or leg
has been; or the way our own shadows
force presence upon us, and bring us back
to the real, when we would have forgotten
ourselves, or have hoped to escape, or to die.

*

Today, the postcard I asked you to send
came—picturing this place so long
seen only in imagination. It is different
from what I'd always imagined, more
monochromatic, both city and sky bathed
in a creamy grayish-brown light flooded
over everything, as in an old sepia drawing.
I wonder if this was only the light, late,
on one unusual afternoon, or whether
it is, there, always, ever afternoon?

*

The city itself, situated high on a hill
or hills, its rocca, its triple ring of defensive
walls, fenced in by a string of sentinel-like
cypresses in the near foreground, seems
almost to float off into the sky. The tall
windowless towers, built for defense,
three with clearly visible *campanili*, thrust
up phallic-like into the ocher air. The sturdy
stone houses on the steep-stepped streets
seem piled almost on top of one another
as they spill down the long sleeve of hill
to huddle and cringe below those lofty
towers. Their large open-eyed windows
stare, like children anywhere, at visitors
from afar.

I recognize the Palazzo del Popolo
on the Piazzo del Duomo, the large medieval
town hall at the top of the hill in the center
of the city—its tower, belfry and steeple the tallest,
the most beautiful, in this *città delle belle torri*.
The castellated roof, ridged with a parapet,
its crenels and merlons above the decorative
fringe of machicolation, makes clear how,
at one time, there was little difference here
between sacred and secular. In the Sala
di Dante below, I know, is the poet's
inscriptive plea, *circa* 1300, to save the city.

*

In the message space you've written the date
and
New Year's
Day
and then added: "There was snow on the ground
when we arrived . . . a rarity; just for me,

I guess." Reading this, I'm stunned to discover
you using almost exactly the same words
I'd used, just a week ago, in a letter to my brother.

You mention a New Year's Eve party you've
stumbled into and out of the night before,
and added some other brief news, then signed
yourself "William" (adding in a parenthesis)
"as they call me here." The card itself has been
addressed by Kate. Knowing no Italian, she
has substituted, in Spanish, "*El Padre de Bill*."

*

The postcard arrived on the very same
day that, ten years ago, my mother died.
It was an overcast day, like today, and we
stood together and alone, in snow and silence,
as if separated by a very great distance.

HOME FROM THE FACTORY

After dinner, before he took
to his books, my father
opened his magnetized

knife and pulled tiny pieces
of metal from his fingers.
Small bubbles of blood

dotted his hands, reddening
the pages of the books I inherited,
and have now finally read.

THE VOYEUR

He has taken up his station
outside the window where he nightly waits.
She often fails, or just forgets,
to close the curtains—or is it
that she knows he is out there, that she
thinks of him the way he thinks of her?

She has begun the process of her slow
undressing, a little ritual that she
seems to take so much delight in.
The light is dim. She has turned her
back. Then, one by one, she smoothly slips
out of all of her things,

dropping them negligently to the floor
around her feet. And then there she is
in all her nakedness. She runs
her hand through her long hair and pauses,
her head half turned toward him,
as if she has heard something,

or seen something beyond the window.
But then, in a moment, she returns
to herself and steps across the softly carpeted floor
toward the bathroom door—and he
has lost her. He has his patience and will watch
and wait for her to return. He can almost

hear the water falling on her everywhere,
almost imagine the small song
she hums, making it up as she goes along,
almost see her taking the towel
to wrap around herself
as she steps from the shower to the cold, tiled

floor. Perhaps she will stop and stand
before the full-length mirror
and see herself as he sees her,
a creature who could walk naked
through many men's dreams,
before she turns and falls asleep with her own.

WINTERSET

Let's say it is winter with a heavy fog hanging low
over a pond in the midst of a stand of trees—oaks
and maples mostly—which have already shed
their leaves and tonged the air. There is a touch
of snow over everything. But someone must be
there to see it, to say it is so, if you are to believe it.

So let's say that. But who is doing the seeing?
Someone would want to know. Is it someone you
have seen perhaps, once or twice, in the small village
you live near, someone you have wondered about,
or been afraid of? And is this person coming
toward you male or female? Which are you?

His breath is like a long scarf thrown over his
shoulder. Her long legs are laced in hip boots.
He/she is coming closer and closer. You have
stopped, stood still, held your breath, wondering
if you've been seen, wondering what you will
say if you are spoken to, wondering what she

is doing out so early on such a morning, wondering
if he has been wondering the same things with
reference to you. Then, inexplicably, not fifty feet
away, the other turns abruptly aside, without
seeming to see you, and slowly climbs the small
steep hill on the other side of the pond and vanishes.

And, after a while, you know that you will too.

THE DIFFERENCE BETWEEN ART AND ARTIFICE

For years, even before you were dead,
I'd envied you, the way you'd been able to
use loss by turning it into art, making it

more than yours, making it ours as well.
Now that you are no longer here, I think that we
are all somewhat confused by what to do,

how to go on without the kind of direction
you gave us—seemingly without your even
knowing it. I remember the time that we all

saw an accident—how immediately you began
to use the details, beyond what was there,
to make it mean in memory when we returned

to revisit it again, even years later. You made
it ours, and art, all at once, more present and
distant simultaneously, so that if we talked

about it later, we could make it mean in a way
we could understand, a way that we hadn't
understood at the time. And, somehow, that

both saved it in real life, as it were, and also
it made it truer than life—as if it had been
memorably illustrated and hung in a gallery,

or placed in a studio, or written down in a poem.

THE LAST TEAM

Dan and Queen were his last team.
I remember them standing stolidly
in their stalls with tired eyes, or slogging
slowly through the slanted morning
light, or, of an afternoon, returning to
the barn after a long day in the fields
with a plow or the old wooden wagon,
their tufted feet raising small bombs
of dust with every step, their ears twitching
in the wind, their tails and manes tossing,
slobber dripping from their drooling
mouths. Then, as if they hadn't already
done enough, we often asked for rides.
Uncle John would go to the barn and bring
them out again to take us round and
around the circle of the driveway. We
would hold to their manes, tighten our
knees on their flanks, stroke their strong
necks, and call them softly by their names
—as I do now: O Dan, O Queen.

NEAR THE CABIN

I had seen the trail of fresh blood
across the edge of the field in front
of the house, but was surprised
when the hunters came to the door
to ask if they could cross the land
and find the deer they knew they
had hit but not killed. I thought
briefly what to say to them and
sent them away. And then I knew
that now it was up to me.

I followed the bursts of the blood
that seemed to have fallen with
each breath. At first there was a
steady trail of the blood, just as there
were traceable tracks, and then
there was less and less of both, each
blood spurt smaller and further apart,
each print fainter and less distinct.
Near the end there was only a bloody
smear, here and there, on a bush
or spotting a stone. And then there
was nothing at all. I went on, in what
seemed the logical direction, and had
almost given up, when, suddenly,
there she was, crumpled over her own
useless legs, staring directly at me,
her chest heaving hard, bubbles of
blood ballooning from her nostrils
and oozing from her opened mouth.
Her eyes were going wild in every
direction at once. Still, she didn't
seem to be afraid.

We stared at one another.
Then she tried to lift herself, and fell.
I didn't know what I could do and
thought I should have left the hunters
to follow, to find her, and finish her
off, to take away what they wanted.

Now, it was just the two of us together.
I sat down on a log far enough away
to keep her calm and watched her,
as she watched me. She seemed to know
that I too could wait, that I didn't want
to harm her further, that neither of us
really knew what to do.

AN EARLY NOVEMBER MEDITATION

The banks have been processing
repossessions and this has caused
me to think about all that I have,
and whether I would want to lose
any of it. Some things, of course,
could easily go and my wife would
be happy about that, and probably
even help me get rid of the piles
and piles of papers and the stacks
and stacks of books in my study,
where she says you can hardly walk
anymore for all the clutter. I have
to agree that it is cluttered and all
of the bookshelves are overfull,
many of them even double-shelved,
but I also know that I know where
everything is, even if I have to look
for it sometimes for hours at a time,
and then often only find it days later
when I am looking for something
else. Then there are all the small
inconspicuous things that even I
only wonder over occasionally:
a paper flying figure that my son
made for me when he was six or
seven, a pair of Korean wedding
dolls given to my wife and me
when we got married, six plastic
chessmen from the famous ivory
Lewis set discovered in Uig Bay
in 1831 and put on permanent
display in the British Museum,
a photograph of my parents
at seventy-five, the only good
likeness I have of the two of them
together, a collection of small

rocks I found in various locations
and lugged home and arranged
in an awkward row, a small wooden
box that I made for my mother
in art class in grade school, painted
with red flowers, which I found
when I was cleaning out the old
house after my parents were dead
—these and so much more. Every
year at about this time, when I am
taking a mental inventory, I think
about these things and wonder
where the years have gone and
about everything I didn't do during
the past years, and I also remember
how it seemed so important to my
parents that I make more rational
decisions about my life, even when
I was too young to make rational
decisions about almost anything.
And I wonder too what the girls
I knew saw in me back then when
we hardly knew anything about life
or what our future might hold for us,
if we were to have one, with one war
going on and another looming and
nothing much looking very good
from where we were, the way we
looked at it, and even really little
things that, at the time, seemed so
huge and how, now, curiously, they
have come back to haunt me more
often than I might have imagined—
things like the death of my dog
when I was six, or how, in an accident
I saw, two men were killed instantly
and another one walked away completely
unharmed, or my first experience with
sex and how confused it caused me

to be for days afterwards, or my favorite
black shooter that I'm sure my best
friend stole on a rainy afternoon the
summer we were ten or eleven and
how we fought about it, wrestling
on the grass in the backyard, both of us
ending up totally exhausted, with no
decisive victory on either side. All
these, and so many more things haunt
me—things I've put away to keep, or
things I've hidden, hoping I will never
have to find them again.

A WALK AROUND THE BLOCK

Years ago, when we started this routine,
we did it for good reasons we could name.
Now, every day, we still take our walk
around the block without much thought.
I guess it's a little like the way a clock
we never notice wears away the hours
and days by telling time while taking it
away. And since the dog died there is less
we have to do, less to think about. I've
noticed, recently, unless you take my hand
or I take yours, that you always walk
a pace or two ahead of me. When I speed
up and try to pull abreast, you increase
your step, dart off, and pull away again.
I've tried to think of this philosophically,
and made of such a little matter much—
much too much, I know you'd say. Still,
just the other day, you said I'd followed
you for years. Now I wonder if you meant
it literally. And so we make our rounds,
nodding to neighbors we almost know,
make small talk, recite the weather. And
when we come to the top of our short hill,
turn the corner and come back home again.

A VISIT

High on the hill, near the barren stands
of oaks and maples, the small pupil
of the pond glints and closes in the late

afternoon light. I have come to stand
and stare off into this distance, across
these stubbled fields fallen fallow

for the winter. The wind hints that
the promise of snow will come before
full dark. I raise my collar and tuck

in the ends of scarf around my throat,
choking off my own blown breath.
I have come back, after years away,

for something I've wanted and waited
to say, but have almost forgotten.
Now, standing still on this small hill,

the icy wind stinging my face, I see
a hawk dive, then quickly rise with
a day's prey twisting in its talons,

a red ribbon of blood trailing beneath
them as they glide up over the trees
and out of sight. There is nothing more

to see or hear. Even the wind is down
to its least whisper. Before me, deep
in their frozen plots, my parents lie

together and alone. I say no prayer, but,
as I linger here, I see how everything
is becoming a beautiful white blindness.